FLORIDIANS ALL

by George S. Fichter
Illustrated by George Cardin

PELICAN PUBLISHING COMPANY
GRETNA 1991

For Nadine

Library of Congress Cataloging-in-Publication Data

Fichter, George S.
    Floridians all / by George S. Fichter ; illustrated by George
Cardin.
      p.   cm.
    Summary: Reviews the lives and accomplishments of people
who were either born in Florida and achieved greatness elsewhere,
or came to Florida and achieved greatness there.
    ISBN 0-88289-804-3
    1. Florida--Biography--Juvenile literature. [1. Florida-
-Biography.] I. Cardin, George, ill. II. Title.
CT229.F53 1991
909'.0982'3--dc20
                                         91-9858
                                           CIP
                                             AC

Manufactured in the United States of America

Published by Pelican Publishing Company, Inc.
1101 Monroe Street, Gretna, Louisiana 70053

PREFACE

Who qualifies as a famous Floridian? What are the criteria used for their selection?

Born in Florida, and therefore a true native? Nearly all of those written about in the following pages would be ruled out if this were the case. Juan Ponce de Leon, whom everyone identifies with Florida, would not be found here. Osceola, the most famous of the Seminoles, would be excluded, too. Only five of the twenty famous Floridians highlighted here are truly natives of the state.

A permanent residency in Florida? Hardly. Again, from the Spanish explorers to the 20th-century shapers of this beautiful state, this would eliminate most of those included in the book. Henry Flagler, the man who opened the east coast of Florida to development from St. Augustine to Key West, was born in New York state. Marjorie Kinnan Rawlings, whom some would call Florida's most gifted observer and spokesperson, came from Washington, D.C.

All of the people written about made a significant impact on their society, and they did it all either for Florida or from Florida. The range of categories is broad — exploration, government, invention, literature, development, entertainment; it is so wide-ranging, in fact, that it becomes difficult to justify why others have not been included. Florida's heritage in all fields of endeavor is rich, and the contributions continue. Many notables have spent — and still spend — much of their lives in Florida simply because of its healthful climate, but not all of them have a solid identification with the state. If they were all included, however, the book you now hold comfortably in your hands would be a hefty piece of work indeed.

7

This, then, is only an introduction to the many people who have achieved fame either for or from Florida. It is hoped that this brief overview will encourage you to find out more on your own about the dynamic people who have contributed to making the state what it is today.

FLORIDIAN ALL

MARY McCLEOD BETHUNE

MARY McCLEOD BETHUNE was born in South Carolina, the fifteenth child of parents who had been slaves. When she was very young, she often went to the home of a white family for whom her mother worked, and she noted that people who had money and who lived comfortably were also those who had an education. She prayed that she would be able to get an education herself. She wanted to learn to read and also to add, subtract, and multiply. At that time this seemed like an impossible dream, for the only school for black people was more than 300 miles from where she lived.

Mary's prayers were answered when a black missionary visited her home, recruiting students for a new school started not far away. Patsy, her mother, decided Mary should be the one in the family to go because she seemed "different" from the other children. Sam, her father, thought she should go because she was exceptionally bright. Both parents recognized that Mary was not cut from the same cloth as everyone else.

Mary attended the school every day, walking five miles each way, and when she got home in the evening, she shared what she had learned with the other members of her family. Soon she had completed her studies at the school and was once again working with her mother. She was the champion cotton picker in the family, regularly picking 250 pounds or more each day. But picking cotton was not what Mary intended to do with her life. Once again she prayed that she could continue her education in some other school. What she had learned only made her thirst for more.

Mary was now fifteen years old, and once again her prayers were answered. This time the answer came in the form of a scholarship to a seminary school in Concord, North Carolina, and she did so well there that she received a second scholarship that sent her to the Moody Institute in Chicago. Upon graduating, she hoped to become a missionary in Africa, but there were no openings at the time. She returned to South Carolina, where she began teaching. Soon she was married and bore a son, Albert.

In the late 1800s, Mary McLeod Bethune moved to Florida — first to Palatka on the St. Johns River and then to Daytona Beach. Henry Flagler was building his railroad southward along the coast. Many of his workers were black, and when Mary observed the poor conditions under which they were living, she related it, as she had in her own case, to a lack of education. She turned her attention to trying to give them the kind of help and opportunities she had received from learning to read. She became an effective missionary among her people, building bridges between blacks and whites where none had existed before.

In 1904, Mary McLeod Bethune opened the Daytona Educational and Industrial Training School for Negro Girls in a small shack in Daytona Beach. At the time she had only $1.50 as financial backing for the venture, but she had no doubt that she would succeed. In the beginning she was not only the head of the school but also its only teacher. At first there were just five students, each of whom paid fifty cents a week for a curriculum of reading, writing, and religion. Two years later the enrollment had increased to 250.

To escape the high cost of renting buildings, Mary McLeod Bethune decided to build her own. For the site she bought an abandoned dump. Then she rolled up her sleeves and started the real work — getting the necessary money together for the construction of the school. Mary described herself as an honest beggar with a good cause. From such wealthy whites as John D. Rockefeller and James A. Gamble, and also from such fund-raising projects as singing with her students and the making and selling of sweet-potato pies and other tasty items, she got the money needed to change the dump into a landscaped campus with a number of buildings.

Recognition for her good work showered on her in the years to come. She received a total of eleven honorary doctorates from prestigious institutions throughout the nation, and she was recognized the world over as an outstanding educator and a crusading civil rights leader. She was an advisor to five presidents of the United States, and she traveled throughout the world, getting more honors everywhere she went.

To Mary McLeod Bethune, who died in 1955, life was a fulfilling adventure. She overcame many obstacles to achieve her status as one of the best-known women in Florida and one of the most respected and influential in the nation. She was an unquestioned success as a parent, teacher, and administrator.

NAPOLEON BONAPARTE BROWARD

. . . a governor of the people

NAPOLEON BONAPARTE BROWARD, Florida's nineteenth governor, was a descendent of a French soldier who had fought in the American Revolution, then settled in what was then Spanish Florida. There he acquired in 1816 a large tract of land. When Napoleon Bonaparte Broward was born in 1857 in Duval County, where Jacksonville is located, the family was well off by the standards of the time.

Tragedy came first in the form of the Civil War. Early in the conflict, the family's slaves left, their buildings were burned, and the fields lay fallow. The farm was sold at a great loss. After the war the family moved westward to Hamilton County, where Napoleon worked with his father and brother in building a log cabin and clearing land for cultivation. The new land was not productive, and the family grew poorer.

Then came more tragedy. Napoleon's mother died in 1869, and his father in 1870. During his teenage years, Napoleon lived with uncles and aunts, and he received only a meager formal education. At a young age, however, he was earning his own way in life. He began working as a crewman on boats plying the St. Johns River, and he rose quickly to become a captain and then a pilot. Later he owned boats himself.

Broward's first wife died in childbirth in 1883. Four years later he married again, and his second wife bore nine children — eight daughters and one son. By 1888, when he was in his early thirties, he began his years serving the public, for the governor appointed him to fill an unexpired term as the sheriff of Duval County. Later that same year he lost the position in an election. Four years later he ran for sheriff and won, but he was soon removed from office on the charge

15

of having police and deputies interfere with a local election. Undaunted, he ran for the office again in 1896. He won, and this time he remained in office.

All the while, Broward's popularity was increasing. As a result of his work with boats on the St. Johns River, he was well known over a large area of Florida. With his brother and a friend, he built and operated a boat called *The Three Friends*. It was designed for towing and also for carrying passengers and freight between Jacksonville, Florida and Nassau in the Bahamas, but soon it was carrying men, guns, and ammunition to Cuban rebels who were trying to force the Spaniards out of Cuba. The trips taken by *The Three Friends* were dangerous but highly profitable.

In 1900, Broward won a seat in the state legislature. A few years later he ran for governor and was elected. As a Liberal Democrat, he promoted himself as the representative of the people — as the champion of farmers, cattlemen, small businessmen, and labor. As governor, he did indeed attend to the needs of these people and also to achieving a better public education system. Unquestionably he worked for what he believed to be best for the state and its people.

Some of Broward's numerous proposals were unusual and were not accepted. One, for example, was a suggestion that all of the property owned by blacks be bought and then a black nation established, in this way guaranteeing them their complete independence. Among his accepted "firsts," however, were the establishment of a pure food law, making it illegal either to sell or to give cigarettes to minors, initiation of a speed law for automobiles, and the requirement that all automobiles be registered with the state.

One of Broward's most ambitious undertakings has since become recognized as a major error. He wanted to open up south Florida for farming and settlement. To do this meant massive drainage of the lowlands, particularly in the Everglades region. The programs he initiated to accomplish this

16

objective were still in action for decades after he was no longer governor, and their negative effects on the ecology of the region are still felt today.

Broward became governor when people wanted change and reform in their government. He delivered both. Because of his many programs, Broward is ranked as one of the state's most constructive governors. When his term as governor was over, he ran for the U.S. Senate, but he died before the election.

In 1915, Broward County — where Fort Lauderdale is located on Florida's lower southeast coast — was established and named in Napoleon Bonaparte Broward's honor.

LEROY COLLINS

LeROY COLLINS worked in a general store when he was a young boy. One day as he was sweeping the floor, the handle of his broom knocked a jar of jelly off the shelf. The glass cracked, and so the jar could no longer be sold.

To teach young LeRoy to be more careful, the storekeeper told him he would have to pay for the jelly. The price was not high, but it would nevertheless take a significant bite out of LeRoy's small pay. LeRoy did some quick thinking. With a bit more money he bought a loaf of bread and then made jelly sandwiches to sell to the store's customers. Even at a bargain price, the sandwiches boosted what had been a loss into a handsome profit.

Fortunately for Florida, LeRoy Collins did not go into the fast-food business, at which he would surely have been a success. Instead he entered public service, where he exercised the same sort of quick thinking and wisdom for the benefit of the people. In Florida, he was first a representative, then a senator, and finally a governor. Then he became president of the National Association of Broadcasters, and after that he returned to public service by serving as Undersecretary of Commerce for the United States government.

Born in Tallahassee in 1909, LeRoy Collins grew up in the state's capitol when it was very much a part of the traditional Old South. The town had only a few more than 5,000 inhabitants. The entire state had only about 700,000, with most of the population concentrated along the Georgia and Alabama borders.

LeRoy was the fourth child in a family of six. While he was young, LeRoy was kept busy with family chores, and even when there was time for himself, he worked at the grocery store and sold boiled peanuts and newspapers on the steps of the capitol. He probably never dreamed at that time that he would one day be the state's chief executive.

His mother hoped he would become a Methodist minister, like his grandfather, but when LeRoy Collins did select a profession, he decided on law. He received his law degree from a university in Tennessee. When he returned to Tallahassee, he was soon elected as the state representative of Leon County. The year was 1935, and LeRoy Collins was 26 years old. This was the beginning of a political career that he would continue for more than a quarter of a century.

The public-service career was interrupted during World War II, when LeRoy Collins served in the U.S. Navy. Back in Tallahassee again, he once more became a legislator. He was a senator when he was elected to fill the unexpired term of Governor McCarty, who had died in office. He was then reelected for a full term, winning in the first primary over five opponents for the Democratic nomination. In all, he served as the state's chief executive officer from 1955 to 1961. He became the first governor since the Civil War to be nominated as permanent chairman of the Democratic National Convention.

LeRoy Collins has been described as being "hip deep in personality," an attribute that he did not abuse but certainly used to his advantage. He was the first Florida governor to make major use of the press, radio, and television for getting his messages to the people. He talked to the people regularly, telling them what he was doing and why, and he asked their opinions about what should be done to guide the state forward.

He acknowledged that change was due in Florida — that it must be done even though it would be difficult. He was opposed to immediate integration, a big issue of the time, because he felt it would be harmful to both sides. He promoted and achieved a slower-paced but harmonious integration. Under his leadership, Florida's school systems were strengthened at all levels.

In his day, LeRoy Collins was a liberal when liberalism was long overdue. Today he might wear the label of conservative. But no matter what he might be called, there was general agreement then — and would also be now — that LeRoy Collins did what was best for the people and their state. He was an outstanding governor who moved Florida forward on all fronts.

MARJORIE STONEMAN DOUGLAS

MARJORIE STONEMAN DOUGLAS was born in Minneapolis in 1890, then spent her early years in Rhode Island and Massachusetts. She graduated from Wellesley, and after a short, unsuccessful marriage, she moved to the small town of Miami, Florida in 1915 to work with her father, Frank Stoneman, who had started a newspaper called *The Herald*. She did regular reporting, wrote occasional fiction and drama, and was also an early champion of equal rights for women.

In 1924 Marjorie Stoneman Douglas began making her living as a free-lance writer, doing fillers and short stories for a number of magazines — most notably the *Saturday Evening Post*. She did well, but her real days of triumph were still in the offing.

A friend who was editor of the Rivers of America series suggested that she might do a book about the Miami River. Marjorie Stoneman Douglas did not know much about rivers, but she did know that the Miami River, with its origin in the Everglades, was very short and hardly seemed qualified in any manner for the treatment deserved by such historic waterways as the Ohio, Missouri, Mississippi, and others. But the idea of doing a book fascinated her. She was at that time working off and on on a novel, but here was a real expressed interest in her work. She began to research the possibilities.

To Marjorie Stoneman Douglas, the Everglades gradually did become a river — a massive sheet of water creeping steadily southward over the tip of the state. She immortalized this concept in her book *The Everglades — River of Grass*, which was first published in 1947 but is so important and timeless that it is still in print. It implanted the Everglades firmly in the minds of people throughout the state, the nation, and the world.

Until the publication of that book, the Everglades was looked on as nothing but a useless swamp — a vast watery world that bred mosquitoes and was a haven for alligators and other wild creatures. It was considered fit only to be drained and reclaimed, a process that had been underway since about 1900. But even Marjorie Stoneman Douglas did not become seriously involved in saving the Everglades until 20 years after her book was published. By this time she was 78 years old.

Ecology was slowly becoming a household word. People now were beginning to understand the importance of protecting the environment and were particularly concerned about the value of such fragile wetlands as the Everglades. Even so, they were not as strong as those who were still destroying the environment. What stirred Marjorie Stoneman Douglas into a relentless fight for the Everglades was her involvement with the National Audubon Society. They wanted her help in stopping the building of a jetport that would have disrupted the Everglades ecosystem irreparably. At their encouragement, she started the Friends of the Everglades and soon had some 3,000 members in nearly 40 states. Marjorie Stoneman Douglas, a tiny, elderly woman wearing a floppy hat, became a familiar spokesperson at meetings throughout the state and even in the nation's capitol. She pulled no punches. She gathered her facts, decided what was right, and then insisted that no alternate course be taken. The jetport was stopped.

But Marjorie Stoneman Douglas continued her work. The preservation of the Everglades was and is an on-going project. In recognition of her tireless efforts, state lawmakers named the headquarters for the Department of Natural Resources in Tallahassee the Marjorie Stoneman Douglas Building. This small woman took on a big mission at a time in her life when others her age and many much younger were doing nothing. Let us hope for Florida's sake that there will be others like her.

HENRY FLAGLER

HENRY M. FLAGLER was already a rich man when he moved to Florida, but in Florida he became even richer.

He was born in 1830 in Hopewell, New York, and spent his boyhood in small New York villages. As a young man he moved to northeastern Ohio. He was almost 30 years old when Edwin Drake opened the first oil well in the nation along the Allegheny River in Pennsylvania. He saw great possibilities in the use of oil and, most particularly, in its marketing. With John D. Rockefeller, he founded an oil company that became organized as the Standard Oil Company. They brought uniformity to the chaos of the many small refineries, and in a little more than a decade after its formation, the Standard Oil Company controlled roughly 95 percent of the oil refineries in the United States and throughout the world.

Henry Flagler was 53 years old when he first visited St. Augustine, Florida. He was appalled by its lack of comfortable facilities for hosting visitors. All of Florida, in fact, represented an investment challenge to him. It was a frontier of opportunities and needs. Flagler withdrew as an active daily participant in the Standard Oil Company and moved to Florida, where he began putting both his business wisdom and his money into action.

In St. Augustine, Flagler soon built the luxurious Ponce de Leon Hotel, where tourists were accommodated in plush surroundings. Later he added the lower-priced Alcazar Hotel. These were part of a chain of hotels that eventually extended from St. Augustine to Key West. Before he could expect people to use a hotel, however, Flagler had to make it convenient for them to get to it, and so he began also to build railroads.

Until then, travel in Florida was primarily by ships along the coast or by boats up and down the St. Johns River. Most of Florida's east coast, with its magnificent beaches, was inaccessible and uninhabited. Flagler's railroads, which when consolidated became the Florida East Coast Railroad, opened the east coast of Florida to tourists and to settlers.

By 1892, Flagler had rail service from St. Augustine to New Smyrna. Two years later the railroad stretched as far south as Palm Beach, where Flagler later built the famous Royal Poinciana Hotel. By 1896, the railroad extended as far south as Miami.

Then, in 1905, Flagler began his most ambitious project — a railroad hopscotching the islands from Miami to Key West. In places the railroad literally had to "go to sea," at one point spanning some seven miles of open water. Completed in 1912, the railroad was built at a cost of $50 million. The workers — about 4,000 in all — were a motley crew of Greeks, Bahamians, Italians, Caymanders (people from the Cayman Islands), and others. Their pay was low, and the working conditions were both difficult and dangerous. Some 700 workers lost their lives.

Plagues of mosquitoes and sand flies drove many off the job, but the most dreaded hazard was hurricanes. Without warning systems, hurricanes were upon them before they were aware of their approach. There was neither time to get away nor an escape route. Three times — in 1906, 1909, and 1910 — these powerful storms were so devastating they nearly halted the project, but Henry M. Flagler insisted on its completion and participated in the dedication ceremony for the railroad in Key West.

The following year — in 1913 — Henry M. Flagler died. He had spent most of his last days in Whitehall, his mansion in Palm Beach. He was interned in a mausoleum alongside the Flagler Presbyterian Church that he had built in St. Augustine.

For many years the paths he had forged through the state were followed by countless thousands. His hotels hosted untold numbers of these visitors, and his railroads carried untold tons of freight. His railroad that "went to sea" went *into* the sea in a 1935 hurricane. It was totally destroyed and was never rebuilt. The Overseas Highway along which automobiles and trucks travel today follows its path.

JONATHAN GIBBS

JONATHAN GIBBS was born of free parents in Philadelphia about 1827. Gibbs graduated from Dartmouth College in 1852, then studied for two more years at Princeton Theological Seminary. He held positions as a Presbyterian pastor in New York and Pennsylvania, then opened a mission and school for freed blacks in North Carolina. He soon started a similar sort of mission in Florida to do charitable work among the blacks.

As a Republican, he was one of the 46 delegates to the Constitutional Convention in 1868. Eighteen of the delegates were black. Most of the delegates, both black and white, were barely literate, making Gibbs decidedly an exception. He was certainly the most cultured gentleman in the delegation. That same year he was appointed by Florida's governor, Harrison Reed, to be secretary of state.

Jonathan Gibbs was outstandingly effective in his work and was highly respected by nearly all members of the Republican Party. The work was both challenging and difficult, and there were still many people opposed to the freedom granted the slaves by the Civil War. Among the most radical were the members of the Ku Klux Klan, and throughout northern Florida more than 200 people, both blacks and whites, were murdered. When in 1871 a highly respected former county clerk was shot in Marianna, Florida, the outspoken Jonathan Gibbs suggested that he should be honored as one of the two Floridians to be immortalized in the Statuary Hall of Fame in Washington. (His proposal was not accepted. John Gorrie and Edmund Kirby-Smith are represented there rather than the Marianna martyr.)

In recognition of his superb leadership, in which he did not let either race or politics dictate his decisions, Governor Reed appointed Jonathan Gibbs to the position of superintendent of public instruction in 1873. Roughly a third of Florida's 200,000 people were illiterates at the time, and about three fourths of them were black. Jonathan Gibbs immediately set about bettering the opportunities for education and the quality of what was offered for both blacks and whites. He established a standard selection process for textbooks throughout the state. He also began in-depth studies of ways to increase educational offerings. Funding for education was lamentably low, and trained teachers were scarce, partly because of the low pay, but also because of poor teaching facilities. School terms were less than six months each year. There were still strong feelings in Florida, too, that education should not be provided to blacks at state expense. Jonathan Gibbs had his work cut out for him.

Gibbs felt that he was seeing progress, however. "Men bitterly opposed to the school system a few years ago, regarding it as a political hobby to be used for party purposes, now see the necessity of educating the masses and willingly cooperate in school work," he said in a speech given to the National Education Association in Elmira, New York in August, 1873.

A year later Gibbs died suddenly and somewhat mysteriously. It was rumored that he was actually poisoned by someone who could not tolerate his demanding style of leadership. Gibbs had indeed blazed a trail in a virtual wilderness. People throughout the state mourned the loss of one of their most valued citizens and one of the best friends ever of their public school system. His work has been recognized by having high schools and a major building at Florida A & M University in Tallahassee named after him.

LUE GIM GONG

LUE GIM GONG was born near Canton in China where, as a child, he worked on his father's farm. He left China when he was entering his teenage years, sailing from Hong Kong and landing at San Francisco. Immediately he set out across the continent, earning his way as he went.

At North Adams, Massachusetts, his independence and high intelligence won the attention of well-to-do Fanny Burlingame, and she adopted him unofficially. Lue Gim Gong quickly learned English and also became well acquainted with the democratic way of government. With four Chinese students at a meeting near Philadelphia in the early 1880s, he drew up a plan for a Chinese republic. His four companions elected Lue Gim Gong as president. China, however, never heard what the five young men proposed.

Lue Gim Gong could not tolerate the cold Massachusetts winters, and a Boston doctor said he did not have long to live. In 1886, he went back to China for a reunion with his family, but homesickness for his American friends soon sent him back to the United States. This time he moved with the Burlingames to a country home near DeLeon Springs in Florida, and on five acres of land given him by the Burlingames, he began the horticultural work that would bring him acclaim as the Luther Burbank (a famous American botanist) of Florida.

Lue Gim Gong had been taught the art of pollination by his mother, and to this he added the skill of cross-pollinating to get wholly new varieties of fruits and vegetables. He concentrated most of his work on citrus. Among the new varieties that he developed was an orange that remained on the

35

tree until it was ripe rather than falling prematurely as did most oranges at that time. This earned him the Wilder Medal from the United States Department of Agriculture, for it was estimated that the new fruit would save the citrus industry countless millions of dollars. Lue Gim Gong also developed a grapefruit that could withstand several degrees of lower temperature than could the grapefruit commonly grown, another huge savings for the industry in those winters when cold fronts pushed into the Florida peninsula. The perfumed grapefruit, another new variety, was not edible, but it gave off a pleasant and permeating fragrance — one ripe fruit filled an entire room with its enhancing aroma.

Citrus fruits were the main focus of Lue Gim Gong's horticultural attention, but he also worked with others. He developed a peach that could be grown in a greenhouse and produce its fruit in late fall — just in time for Thanksgiving meals. He also developed the apple currant, a tree-sized tomato plant bearing clusters of edible tomatoes that were all the same size, and a raspberry like the common raspberry in taste, but salmon colored.

Lue Gim Gong's citrus grove near DeLeon Springs grew in size to 45 acres. When Fanny Burlingame died in 1903, her heirs deeded to him her property and added $12,000 in cash. He graciously accepted, but within a few years had dissipated the money in performing more experiments with plants. "No one should live in the world for self alone, but to do good for those who come after him," he once explained.

Thousands of people visited Lue Gim Gong every year, and he cheerfully toured them through his grove and explained his experiments. He became a Christian in his later years and always took his visitors to his private chapel for a prayer at the end of the tour.

Lue Gim Gong was poor in money but rich in friends when he died in 1925. At one point, people in the community rallied to his aid to pay off a mortgage on his property so that he could continue his work without money worries. In the Florida exhibit at the New York World's Fair in the 1940s, a statue honoring this kindly Chinese plant wizard was displayed.

JOHN GORRIE

. . . doctor and inventor

JOHN GORRIE, one of the two Floridians in the Statuary Hall in the United States Capitol, was a medical doctor and also an inventor. His early life remains a mystery. According to most historians, he was born on October 3, 1803, in Charleston, South Carolina. Others say he was born on the island of Nevis in the West Indies and was brought to South Carolina when he was still a tiny baby. No substantial records exist for proof of either claim.

Who was his father? This is not really known. It is possible, too, that his real name was not Gorrie.

A frequent story is that his mother and her year-old son were dropped off in Charleston by a Captain Gorrie, an officer of Scottish descent in the employ of the Spanish army. Captain Gorrie established a substantial bank account for the woman and then went back to the West Indies. It is not known whether Captain Gorrie was John Gorrie's father, but the woman did give her son his name. She was distinctly Spanish herself, and John Gorrie also looked Spanish. Over the years of his youth, John Gorrie's mother apparently got substantial sums of money periodically so that her son could be given the best possible private education. Where the money came from is not known, but it has been speculated that its origin was with Spanish nobility. When John Gorrie reached manhood, the money was no longer provided, and it became his responsibility also to support his mother.

At age 24, John Gorrie graduated from medical school in New York. His whereabouts for the following several years are not clear, but in 1833 he established his medical practice in the flourishing town of Apalachicola, Florida.

He was not only skillful in his profession but also highly personable. Soon he was serving in various civic positions — as postmaster, on the city council, as director and then president of a bank, and as an investor and participant in a number of business ventures.

After several years, however, Dr. Gorrie gave up on most of these involvements to concentrate on his medical profession. He had become greatly concerned about correcting certain environmental conditions that he felt contributed to his patients' two major medical problems — malaria and yellow fever. He did not know, nor did anyone else of his time, that the diseases were carried by mosquitoes. He suspected that the watery lowlands were largely responsible. He associated the diseases with decaying organic matter, moisture, and heat.

His method of treating patients was achieving control of the temperature in their rooms. To do this, he suspended an ice-filled container from the ceiling and then passed a current of air over it. He was simulating the coolness of a cave, and in the process he was also air-conditioning the room.

A major problem had to be resolved to make air conditioning practical, however, for in Apalachicola the temperature soared in summer and ice was either unobtainable or was much too expensive to be used in cooling rooms. For this reason, Dr. Gorrie set about building a machine to make ice, and he demonstrated the machine publicly in 1850. The patent he received was the first granted in America for the production of ice by mechanical means. Other ice-making machines were patented in the years immediately following, but Dr. Gorrie's was definitely the first. Some of the others, too, were only ideas on paper and were never actually made.

Unfortunately, Dr. John Gorrie was many years ahead of his time. He was unsuccessful in selling his invention to investors for production, though he demonstrated it time and again. It delivered brick-sized chunks of ice, which he made available locally wherever there was a special need. He pointed out that the machine could be made to produce ice continuously and in whatever size desired, but he had no success in generating financial support. Some thirty years would follow before ice-making machines of any sort were in common usage anywhere.

His frustration at his inability to interest investors may have contributed to the illness that brought about his death, recorded as having occurred on June 16, 1855. But was that the right date? His will, presumably signed by him, was dated June 27, 1855. Again, Dr. Gorrie's personal life was a mystery.

His contribution to a better way of life for people everywhere is acknowledged in Apalachicola by a monument to him and by the Gorrie Bridge across the Apalachicola Bay. His name is also in the record books as the inventor of an ice-making machine and air conditioning.

MAY MANN JENNINGS

. . . an early conservation activist

MAY MANN JENNINGS was the wife of Governor William S. Jennings, the state's eighteenth governor. She was Florida's "First Lady" from 1901 to 1905, but her most important and significant achievements were to come later.

Born in New Jersey in 1872, May Jennings was still an infant when her family moved to Crystal River, Florida, where she spent her girlhood. At age eleven she was sent to St. Joseph's Convent in St. Augustine, where she got a thoroughly "southern-style" education. She graduated with honors and was valedictorian of her class. Still in her early thirties when her duties as First Lady were over, she moved with her husband to Jacksonville, where she remained active in civic and political affairs. Most notably she was an organizer of the Duval County Federation of Women's Clubs, president of the Florida Federation of Women's Clubs, and president of the Duval County Democratic Women. It was through these organizations and by exercising her boundless energy and enthusiasm that she engineered long-lasting accomplishments.

At the time of its discovery in 1513, Florida's forests covered some 30 million acres, ranging from the pinelands in the central and panhandle sections of the state through oaks, palmettos, cypresses, mangroves, and the varied subtropical forests in the extreme southern section. Trees were plentiful, and no one had the slightest concern about their preservation or replacement. By 1850, however, most of the pine forests had been cleared for turpentine and lumber and to open the land for farming and grazing. Lumbering then moved southward, and by the turn of the century almost no virgin timber remained anywhere in the state. All of the forests were second growth.

By the 1920s voices of worry began to be heard. May Jennings was among them, and she became a leader in establishing in 1927 the Florida Board of Forestry. It consisted of five members with staggered terms to assure a continuity in thought and programs. The Board was charged with arriving at a fire protection and control program, making information on forest management available, and cooperating with industries and landowners in promoting good forestry practices. The following year Florida's first full-time forester was appointed to work in a newly created state agency — the Florida Forester Service. For her work in bringing about the legislation creating the Board of Forestry, May Jennings has been called the "Mother of Florida Forestry."

Even earlier, May Jennings had piloted the state toward preserving a parcel of the subtropics at the very southern tip of the mainland. Called Paradise Key, its hammock had a stand of magnificent and stately royal palms that stood up to 100 feet tall, their grayish-white trunks looking as though they were made of concrete. Royal palms lined avenues in Fort Myers, Miami, and other cities, but they had been imported from Cuba. Their existence as native trees was not generally known.

May Jennings and her women's clubs initiated a program to create a state park in which the handsome trees would be protected. The state of Florida responded by setting aside about 930 acres of land, and this was then matched by Henry Flagler's Florida East Coast Railroad Company. With this as its beginning, Royal Palm State Park was dedicated in November of 1916. Some 750 people were taken by automobile to the remote and unique hammock in the Everglades for the ceremony. In 1921, the state enlarged the park with more than 2,000 additional acres. Few people visited the difficult-to-reach park, and it was plagued by hurricanes and by fires during the dry season. It was, in fact, a financial failure.

May Jennings was determined to have the land serve the people well. When Ernest Coe, David Fairchild, and others began their efforts to create Everglades National Park, May Jennings was quick to suggest that Royal Palm State Park could become the core of the larger federally owned and operated park. This came to pass, and the royal palms and the land around them assumed a new and productive role. The trees there are admired yet today.

May Jennings died in 1963, after a long and fruitful life. When Stetson University awarded her an honorary doctor of laws degree, the president of the university referred to her as one who had "doctored more laws than anyone else in the state." Her name is still honored throughout the state as a wise conservationist with concerns and accomplishments decades ahead of her time.

JAMES WELDON JOHNSON

JAMES WELDON JOHNSON's father was from Virginia and his mother was from Nassau in the Bahamas but was reared and educated in New York City. They were married in Nassau during the Civil War. When the war was over, they moved to Jacksonville, Florida, where both James Weldon and his brother John Rosamond were born — James in 1871 and John in 1873. Both were highly intelligent and creative. Their mother was the first black teacher in Florida's public schools, and she taught her sons to read before they started school. She also taught both to play the piano and the organ at an early age.

James preferred to spend his time reading and studying, and John found music most satisfying. James had a special liking for cold and rainy weather because on those kinds of days he could stay indoors and read, think, and write. The attic was his private hideaway, and the family respected his desire to be alone now and then.

The Johnson family was poor but proud. Both parents were kind, but they were also firm disciplinarians. James' father worked as the head waiter in the St. James Hotel. In addition to her teaching, his mother did washing, ironing, and other household chores. In this way they maintained a modest but comfortable home in which the children felt secure.

During his boyhood, James Weldon Johnson was not as bothered by discrimination in Jacksonville as were blacks in other parts of the South. Jacksonville had blacks represented in nearly all governmental positions throughout the city, either by appointment or election. It was not until he left Jacksonville that James Weldon Johnson experienced problems with racial prejudice.

When he finished the eighth grade in 1890 at Stanton School, where his mother taught, James had gone as far as he could go at that school and also farther than most blacks of his day. He aspired to do more, and so he enrolled first in a preparatory school and then in Atlanta University. As part of his training he taught among the poorer blacks in rural Georgia, and perhaps more than any other experience in his life, this caused him to ponder what he could do to bring about educational, social, and economic equality for both blacks and whites.

After his graduation from Atlanta University, he returned to Jacksonville, where he became the principal of Stanton School. He made it one of his objectives to expand the school to the high school level, and this was accomplished. At the same time he was studying law on his own, and he became the first black to pass the Florida bar examination. For the better part of a year he also published a newspaper.

John Rosamond, his brother, had turned his attention wholly to music and had gone to Boston to study and to work. He also traveled with a theatrical company. James still had an interest in music, too. In 1900, in commemoration of Abraham Lincoln's birthday, James wrote a song that was sung by a chorus of some 500 schoolchildren. His brother provided the music for the stirring lyrics. Called "Lift Every Voice and Sing," it has since become a standard hymn among blacks.

Despite his already varied and successful career, James Weldon Johnson had a thirst to do still more. He liked to be where things were happening and also to make things happen wherever he went. He moved to New York City, where he worked with his brother in writing songs and producing plays for Broadway. He liked New York very much and soon considered it his home. There, too, he became more involved in pol-

48

itics. He campaigned vigorously for Theodore Roosevelt when he won the presidency in 1906.

At age 35, Johnson joined the United States Consular Service and was sent first to Venezuela and then to Nicaragua. In 1912 he resigned from the foreign service and returned to New York. There he resumed his writing and at the same time became active in the civil rights movement. He served as field director for the National Association for the Advancement of Colored People. Four years later he was named the executive director, a post he held for a decade. He was given a medal for his outstanding service to the organization and the people it represents.

For eight years, James Weldon Johnson was a professor of creative literature at Fisk University and was at the same time listed as a professor at New York University. All during these years he continued to write — poetry, fiction, and nonfiction. *Along This Way*, his autobiography published in 1933, is highly acclaimed. In most of his writings he pointed out that the destiny of blacks depended on what they did themselves and not what other people did for or to them. He continued to be active until his untimely death in 1938 when the automobile he was driving struck a train.

Few have ever achieved success in so many different fields of endeavor, but perhaps James Weldon Johnson's greatest accomplishment was the softening of prejudice between blacks and whites.

BETTY MAE TIGER-JUMPER

. . . moving towards a better future

BETTY MAE TIGER-JUMPER credits her successes to setting goals, achieving them, and then immediately setting new goals.

Betty Mae was born in Indiantown, Florida, on April 22, 1922. Her mother was a Seminole Indian and her father was white. In those years interracial marriages were greatly frowned upon by the Seminoles, and so during her early years Betty Mae was often not accepted by the older Seminoles. She nevertheless maintained complete allegiance to the Seminoles and to bettering their living conditions and their futures.

Late in the 1920s, she moved from Indiantown to the reservation at Hollywood, Florida. While attending a missionary church meeting, she recognized the importance of learning to read. Her parents encouraged her, but her grandparents and other older Seminoles greatly opposed her taking such a step into the outer world. The Cherokee Indian Boarding School she attended in North Carolina was disdainfully labeled a "white man's school." Betty persisted with her education, however, and became one of the first Florida Seminoles to graduate from high school. As the years passed — and with Betty Mae's constant encouragement — going to school began to be taken for granted among her people. The first Seminole to graduate from college was Billy Cypress, who earned a degree from Stetson University in 1965.

Older tribe members were even more critical when Betty Mae decided to become a trained nurse. She went ahead with her plan and enrolled in the Kiowa Indian Hospital nurses' training program in Lawton, Oklahoma. When she returned to South Florida to put her training to good use in health care

51

for her people on the reservation and also those living along the Tamiami Trail in the Everglades, the older members of the tribe at first threw mud on her white uniform. Betty Mae again ignored the disapproval and went about her work, the health of the Seminoles more important to her than her acceptance by the old-timers.

In 1947, Betty Mae Tiger married Moses Jumper. He was one of two Seminoles who fought for the United States in World War II. They had three children — Moses, Jr., Scarlett Jumper-Young, and Boettner. Even while she was busy with her own family, Betty Mae continued to do important work for the Seminoles. Her great contribution was firming their organization as a tribe in 1957. From 1967 until 1971, she served as chairman of their tribal council. One of the prevailing problems was lack of money. Before she became chairman, the council had less than a hundred dollars in its till. She organized profitable enterprises so that the council can now give each tribal member more than a thousand dollars every year.

Even after her retirement from the tribal council, Betty Mae has continued to work at her goals of getting more jobs for Seminoles and of making certain the younger Seminoles have good educational opportunities. Nor has her work been wholly confined to her own tribe or to Florida. In 1969, she was one of the leaders in the formation of the United South and Eastern Tribes, Inc., or USET. Originally only four tribes were represented; now more than a dozen additional tribes have joined, all subscribing to the organization's avowed objective of achieving "strength in unity." USET has been successful in bringing about improved administration, health, and education programs for all of its member tribes.

Keeping her own people well informed has been another persistent goal of Betty Mae. In the 1950s she initiated the *First Seminole News*, which was the first newspaper of the Florida Seminole tribe. Today she continues as editor-in-chief, the publication is now called *The Seminole Tribune*, and she is also director of the communications program.

Billy Cypress describes Betty Mae Tiger-Jumper as "a pathfinder." Certainly she has guided her people to a position of importance and influence in the state and nation.

EDMUND KIRBY-SMITH

. . . last Confederate general to surrender

EDMUND KIRBY-SMITH is one of the two Floridians honored in the Statuary Hall of Fame in Washington, D.C. The other is Dr. John Gorrie.

Born in St. Augustine in 1824 of New England parents, Edmund Kirby-Smith attended West Point, where he was nicknamed "Seminole" by his classmates. There, too, he hyphenated his middle and last names to distinguish himself from the many other Smiths. In 1845 he graduated from West Point as an infantry officer.

During the Mexican War, Edmund Kirby-Smith fought in eight battles, and he advanced in rank to major. After that conflict, he transferred to the cavalry, and he also returned to West Point, where he taught mathematics. In 1861 he joined the Confederate Army, entering with the rank of lieutenant colonel. He fought in a number of battles and was given a command post in the Shenandoah Valley. As a brigadier general, he led the Confederate Army in the first battle of Bull Run and was severely wounded. When he returned to duty, he was advanced to major general and given duty as division commander of the Confederate forces in northern Virginia, and then later in east Tennessee. He led forces in an invasion of Kentucky and achieved a resounding victory at Richmond. This brought about his advancement to lieutenant general.

As a full general he was given command of all activities in Texas, Arkansas, Louisiana, and the Indian Territory — an area totalling some 600,000 square miles that was officially called the Trans-Mississippi Department. This vast domain was virtually isolated from the rest of the country. It became known as Kirby-Smithdom, for with communication as slow and difficult as it was, General Kirby-Smith had to solve problems for himself. He got his own supplies wherever they were available and however it was necessary to get them. He destroyed cotton and other resources to prevent their being utilized by invading forces from the Union, and he ran blockades through Mexico. He even took it upon himself to give field commissions to officers — some to the rank of general. This was done without notification to or approval by President Jefferson Davis. General Edmund Kirby-Smith operated as though he were commanding another country, and in effect this was true.

General Edmund Kirby-Smith did not surrender until May of 1865, the last general of the Confederate Army to do so. After the war Edmund Kirby-Smith did not return to Florida, but he did continue to distinguish himself. First he became president of an insurance company. Following this he was president of the Pacific and Atlantic Telegraph Company. Then he returned to academics, which he liked best, and was appointed president of the University of Nashville. He held that position until 1875, after which he taught mathematics at the University of the South until his death in 1893. He had become the last living full general of the Confederacy.

JUAN PONCE DE LEON

. . . the discoverer of **La Florida**

JUAN PONCE DE LEON was the first governor of Florida. He was neither a Republican nor a Democrat. He was not, in fact, elected to his position. Rather, he became governor by royal command — appointed by King Ferdinand of Spain. Some 75 governors were to follow, most of them Spanish but some British and American, before Florida would have a governor by election.

Juan Ponce de Leon became governor because it was he who discovered Florida. On Easter Sunday, March 27, 1513, he first sighted the land he called *La Florida*. Blown back out to sea by a storm, he was unable to come ashore for six days. Then he and a few soldiers set foot on Florida soil for the first time near the present city of St. Augustine, and he laid claim to the land for Spain. At the time the land was inhabited by only a few thousand Indians in six different tribes. Even the Seminoles had not yet arrived.

Ponce de Leon had first visited the New World 20 years earlier in 1493, when he accompanied Columbus on his second voyage. Juan Ponce de Leon came from a noble family, but the family had lost all of its wealth. At age 15, he offered his services to a highly respected professional soldier and was accepted because he demonstrated both high intelligence and great determination to succeed. Soon he became a page in the King's court. When he was older and began serving in the army, he quickly rose to the rank of captain.

Ponce de Leon had had high hopes for his trip with Columbus because it held promise of enabling him to get back the fortune his family had lost. Gold was unquestionably one of his major goals, as it was for many of his countrymen.

As a soldier he carried out whatever orders came from his superiors, even hunting Indians to make them into slaves or to kill them. To the Spaniards, the Indians were not Christian, and therefore were not human beings. However, Ponce de Leon was throughout his life a man of contrasts. His personal attitudes were frequently quite different, for he was basically kind and understanding, winning his way more with good deeds than with the sword.

At Hispaniola (now Haiti), Columbus had expected to find a flourishing settlement, for when he returned to Spain the previous year, he had left 40 men there. They were putting up buildings when he left. Instead of a thriving settlement, however, he found only charred ruins. From the Indians he learned that the Spaniards had been brutal in their treatment of the Indians, who had at first been submissive but finally could tolerate no more. They destroyed the settlement and killed nearly all of the Spaniards. Those who escaped died in the jungle.

Columbus tried to establish a second settlement, but the Spaniards were more interested in finding gold than in colonizing the land. In the spring of 1496, Columbus returned to Spain, hoping to get an army to assist him. With him he took Captain Juan Ponce de Leon and a troop of soldiers. Six more years passed before Ponce de Leon made his second trip to the New World. Again he traveled to Hispaniola, this time with some 2,500 people. This time, he wanted to try to profit from what the land could produce rather than from gold.

Another six years passed, and Ponce de Leon was doing well with his agriculture. On a report that there was gold in nearby Puerto Rico, he sailed there to investigate for Spain. He did indeed find gold, and he also discovered fertile land that he was sure held great promise for Spain. The Spaniards wanted the gold more than the land, however, and the governor of Hispaniola determined to conquer the Indians and take over the island. Ponce de Leon objected, but with no success.

In time the king of Spain appointed him governor of Puerto Rico. Already the Spaniards had been harsh in their treatment of the Indians, but Ponce de Leon set about mending wounds. During his governorship, Puerto Rico flourished as a Spanish colony. When he lost his position in 1512, Ponce de Leon already had his own land and buildings in Puerto Rico.

One day an old Indian woman came to his house, called Casa Blanca, with a tale about a fountain that had water with magical powers. Drinking or bathing in this water could turn the old into young again. It was not a new story. Many Indians talked about this fountain and its magic water, and they all agreed that it was on an island called Bimini that lay far to the north of Puerto Rico. The old woman said she knew the exact location of Bimini and offered to lead Ponce de Leon to it. The woman was convincing, and Ponce de Leon was fascinated by the story. Possibly he might have thought he could use some water from the fountain himself, for he was 53. Mostly, however, he wanted to find Bimini and lay claim to it for Spain.

Ponce de Leon set sail with three ships on March 13, 1513. Aboard his ship was the Indian woman who was serving as their guide. They sailed through the maze of the Bahama Islands, of which there are some 2,000. Finally, on March 27, the Indian woman said that she saw Bimini, and six days later, after a storm subsided, they finally set foot on what she believed to be Bimini, an island. It was, in fact, Florida. Ponce de Leon himself thought he had discovered a huge island and decided to sail around it. He travelled southward, across the Florida Keys, and then northward along the west coast to Apalachee Bay. He also discovered that the Indians were hostile. Wherever he encountered them, they showed no signs of being friendly and instead sent showers of arrows to greet him.

Home again in Puerto Rico, Ponce de Leon was once more

appointed governor and became involved in fighting the Carib Indians. It was not until 1521 that he was able to return to Florida. This time he was determined to establish a permanent settlement, and he paid for the entire expedition himself. This included two ships on which he carried 200 colonists plus horses, cattle, pigs, sheep, goats, many kinds of seeds, tools, and other necessities. This was to be Florida's first settlement, and Ponce de Leon had elected the west coast for its location because it was closer by ship to both Mexico and Cuba than was the east coast.

The ships sailed into what is now Charlotte Harbor, near present-day Venice. Cautious because of his earlier experience with the Indians of Florida, Ponce de Leon waited for a day and a half before going ashore. He saw no fires or any other signs of Indians. The land here seemed empty and safe, which was precisely as he wanted it.

At last he ordered the ships unloaded. Even before the unloading was completed, Ponce de Leon had men at work cutting trees to build a stockade. He knew that eventually the Indians would come and that they would not be friendly. The stockade would be essential for protection.

What Ponce de Leon did not know was that the Indians were already there, watching his every move. At noon on the second day, they attacked. Arrows flew from bows powerful enough to send them through the armor worn by the Spanish soldiers. Other arrows hit unprotected areas of the soldiers' bodies or some of the people who had come only as colonists and were completely unprotected.

Ponce de Leon stood bravely in the onslaught until he caught an arrow in his thigh. Their leader downed, the Spaniards went into a panic. Quickly they carried Ponce de Leon to a skiff and got him aboard one of the ships. Those still on shore now retreated, too, and soon the ships had pulled anchor and were on their way to Cuba.

The Spanish hoped to get medical help for the wounded Ponce de Leon in Cuba. A thigh wound from an ordinary arrow would not have been serious, but the point of this arrow had been dipped in poison. Even in Cuba there was no help for him, and he soon died.

Juan Ponce de Leon did not discover the fabled Fountain of Youth, but he was the first to make use of the Gulf Stream and the Bahama Channel, both used later by many sailing vessels. He also discovered Florida and laid claim to it for Spain. It remained Spanish property for more than 200 years.

PEDRO MENENDEZ

Fort Caroline

St Augustine

PEDRO MENENDEZ was born in 1519, the year Magellan embarked on his voyage around the world. Menendez himself was destined to pioneer for Spain, for he grew up in those years when Spain was involved in world conquest. Menendez, in fact, became one of King Philip II's key military leaders. He was clever, daring, courageous, and, many feel, ruthless, but he was a master of the seas and of warfare.

In 1564, France established a colony at the mouth of the St. Johns River in Florida. This was Spanish territory, but Spain had not yet made permanent settlements in Florida. The French called their settlement Fort Caroline. Their objective was to find gold and silver, but they found none. Soon the people in the little settlement were near starvation, and some of them set out to sea in a small boat to get back to France. When news of their plight reached France, Jean Ribald was dispatched to Fort Caroline to put the settlement in order again.

Word of the French settlement had also reached Spain, and King Philip commanded Menendez to drive off the intruders. Menendez had been preparing to leave, in fact, at the same time as Jean Ribald. He departed with 30 ships and more than 2,000 people, plus livestock and various tools and other items they would need to establish a permanent colony. A storm scattered the ships, and only nine reached Puerto Rico. Almost immediately Menendez took five ships and about 600 people to continue on to Florida, travelling northward through the Bahamas.

Jean Ribald reached Florida first. The people he brought swelled the Fort Caroline settlement to about 700. Among them were several hundred soldiers whom Ribald would use to fight the Spaniards.

It was about a week later that Menendez landed at what is now St. Augustine and established a settlement there in the name of Spain. This was the first of six that he eventually started in Florida, an achievement that earned him the title of "founder of Florida." But before he could put down more roots, Menendez had to destroy the Fort Caroline settlement to the north of St. Augustine.

Menendez surprised the French by marching overland to Fort Caroline. He attacked and killed nearly all of the several hundred at the fort, sparing only those who were Catholic. He then renamed the settlement San Mateo.

Ribald had taken his soldiers by ship to St. Augustine, which he planned to attack and destroy. Menendez hurriedly returned by his overland route, fully expecting to find St. Augustine completely laid waste. Amazingly, St. Augustine had not been touched. The French ships had encountered a severe storm and had been blown back to sea. Some had been wrecked on an offshore island, and Menendez learned that about 200 soldiers were marooned on an island not far from St. Augustine. With his 50 soldiers, Menendez was far outnumbered, so he decided to overcome the French by trickery.

From across a swift, deep-water pass, Menendez talked to the French in their language and got them to allow him to ferry them to the mainland in a small boat. He picked them up ten at a time and took them behind the dunes on the other side of the pass, where they were run through with swords and their bodies left on the beach. Nearly two weeks later the slaughter was repeated when Menendez found more French- men who had survived the storm at sea but were marooned on the island. Among them was Jean Ribald, and Menendez did not spare his life. To this day the inlet bears the name "Mantanzas," which means "place of slaughter."

With the French eliminated, Menendez set about making friends with the Indians and converting them to Christianity. He also established settlements along both the east and west coasts of Florida. He was not getting the cooperation he needed from Spain to maintain them, however, and four of the six were soon destroyed by hostile Indians.

In Spain, Menendez remained a hero. King Philip made him commander of the nation's mightiest fleet, and he was also the first appointed governor of colonized Florida.

ADDISON MIZNER

. . . he gave Florida its architectural style

ADDISON MIZNER gave Florida its distinctive Spanish-style architecture. When he became very ill at age 46 in 1918, he went to Palm Beach either to recover or to die. In the following decade, he became a legend.

Already he had won and lost several fortunes and had traveled over much of Europe, China, and Central America. He had developed a great interest in both art and architecture and had designed many homes in the New York City area. He had no formal training and could not draw blueprints. Sometimes facilities such as bathrooms and kitchens were not the most functional or convenient. But his designs captured clients — particularly the rich. In Florida, the patterns he set were copied, and soon the face of Florida, from homes of the richest to the poorest, wore the Mizner look.

One of the unique Mizner touches was making his buildings look as though they were a hundred years old rather than glittering new. He took trips to Spain to buy materials from old churches and other buildings. By covering wet concrete with black muck from the swamps and leaving it there until the concrete dried, he gave the finished product a stained, grayish, pitted appearance. He catered to the very rich and charged them very high fees. "These people can't stand the sight of anything that doesn't cost a lot of money," he said.

Mizner also began making roof and floor tiles for his buildings, and he utilized one kiln strictly for producing pottery for his projects. In addition, he made wrought-iron grills, gates, and hardware, plus furniture and lighting fixtures. He became geared up, in fact, to profit on houses all the way from their design stage to when they were furnished and occupied.

The resort areas of South Florida were in their boom years. Money was plentiful, and people were building mansions, the most expensive of them designed by Addison Mizner. Meanwhile, Mizner himself had a special dream — a real colossus. With his brother Wilson he set about creating a city between Palm Beach and Miami at the site of the tiny unincorporated town of Boca Raton. There he bought more than 1,500 acres of land that included two miles of beach. Immediately he began putting out promotional literature about the luxurious new community that would boast a 1,000-room hotel, a street 219 feet wide (enough for 20 lanes of traffic), plus golf courses, parks, and other enticements. Nothing existed at the time, of course, but soon other developers also began working in the area.

Addison Mizner believed in his Boca Raton project just as he did in all of his enterprises, but he had no control over the general economy. In Florida, the land boom ended in 1925. Florida real estate became practically worthless. An era had ended. Addison Mizner again lost a fortune, but his buildings and the style he had created for Florida live on even to this day. Addison Mizner continued to design houses but did not initiate more grandiose real estate developments himself. He died of a heart attack in 1933.

OSCEOLA

. . . proud, defiant leader of the Seminoles

OSCEOLA led the Seminoles in the beginning of the Second
Seminole War that began in 1835. He got his Indian name,
Asi-Yahole, meaning Black Drink Singer, when he was about
18 years old and attained his manhood at a Seminole Green
Corn Dance. Osceola is a corruption of that Indian name.

Osceola was not originally a Seminole. Born in 1804 in Alabama, he first went by the name of Billy Powell. His father
was William Powell, a white trader. His mother was a part-
Indian woman named Polly Copinger, and Osceola moved
with her to Florida when he was about four years old. He
renounced relationship to any white, and following Indian
custom, he allied himself with his mother's kinship and
declared himself to be a Muskogee, a branch of the Creeks.

He stood tall and straight, and during his younger years
he was remarkably athletic. His eyes were light, not dark like
the eyes of most of the Seminoles. Almost arrogantly proud,
he dealt firmly with the whites, but he was never officially
a chief and actually had no voice in their councils. He was
so charismatic, however, his leadership was so strong, and his
words so authoritative that whatever he suggested was followed
by the true Seminole chiefs. It was Osceola who sent this
memorable message to General Clinch: "You have guns, so
have we. You have powder and lead, so have we. Your men
will fight, and so will ours — till the last drop of Seminole blood
has moistened the dust of his hunting ground."

Osceola was recognized for his cunningness, and he was
the acknowledged guiding force behind the Seminoles. He
was both feared and admired. It was Osceola who at Fort King
near present-day Ocala drove his dagger through an offered

treaty and declared, "This is the only treaty I will ever make with the whites."

The military felt that the Seminoles could be subdued only by capturing or killing Osceola and those close to him. However, since this proved impossible for them, his capture was to come by trickery.

Osceola could be ruthless, but he was also reasonable. He had agreed to meet with the whites about 11 miles from St. Augustine. The flag of truce flew over his camp, in which there were some 70 warriors. But as he talked, his encampment was surrounded by four times as many soldiers, under the command of General Thomas S. Jesup. Osceola knew he had been trapped. Turning to a Seminole chief sitting next to him, he said, "You must talk. I am overcome."

The truce flag was still waving when the soldiers closed in. The Seminoles were armed but so vastly outnumbered that they wisely did not attempt to fight. They were marched to St. Augustine and locked up in the old Spanish fort, then called Fort Marion. Everywhere the capture of Osceola was considered a total disgrace, but the fact remained that he was imprisoned and was not to be released. He and his fellow captives were treated well. They were given comfortable places to sleep and were well fed, and they were even permitted to have a ceremonial dance.

Osceola was ill with recurrent malaria plus badly infected tonsils. Others with him planned an escape, but Osceola declined. He was both too weak and too proud to join them. He knew, too, that his family was on the way to the prison, and he did not want them held hostage because of his escape. About 20 of the Seminoles did make it to freedom, however.

Soon Osceola and the remaining prisoners were moved to Fort Moultrie in South Carolina. They arrived on January 1 in 1838, and while Osceola was given especially good quarters, he remained ill and continued to get worse. He met with many visitors in the following days, and he told them how he had been betrayed. He also posed for George Catlin, a noted painter of American Indians, and the two paintings that were done now hang in the Smithsonian Institution in Washington and have been reproduced in countless publications.

Before the end of January, Osceola's condition had deteriorated to the point where he knew he would die. On January 30, the day of his death, he wore his full war dress, perhaps as a symbol to those he left behind that they should carry on. He was 34 years old.

Osceola died in prison, yes, but he also died proudly and undefeated. Neither Osceola nor his people ever surrendered. The chief who became the leader of the Seminoles after Osceola's death echoed his sentiments by declaring that they "had never made a treaty and never would." It was Osceola who had inspired them and given them their independence, defiance, and dignity. To the Seminoles, Osceola was a hero to be honored and emulated, as he is still today.

HENRY PLANT

. . . a pioneer developer

HENRY B. PLANT was one of Florida's pioneer developers. At the same time that Henry Flagler was opening up Florida's east coast with railroads, Henry Plant was busily doing the same thing along Florida's lower Gulf coast and through the central part of the state. Their approaches were slightly different, Henry Plant combining his railroads with steamboat companies that he also owned, but the ultimate results were almost identical.

Henry Plant was born in Branford, Connecticut in 1819. He launched his career in business at age 18 when he began working for a steamboat line that operated between New York City and New Haven, Connecticut. He worked for the company for five years and was offered a position as captain of one of the ships. This he declined, however, because already he had visions of owning and operating his own shipping company. During the Civil War, Plant worked for the Confederacy, organizing their shipping. After the war he became head of the Southern Express Company in Atlanta, and turned his attention to the business frontiers to the south.

In the 1880s, Plant began buying small rail lines in Georgia and northern Florida. At the same time he began joining and extending the lines. One of his first thrusts into southern Florida was a 75-mile new rail line from Kissimmee to Tampa. The rails were laid and the trains running within seven months. He called it the South Florida Railroad, and his objective was making connections with his own steamship service from Tampa to Key West and Cuba. Plant also owned the People's Line, which operated steamboats on the St. Johns River from

Sanford to Jacksonville, where connections were made with his more northern rail lines.

Plant's expansion began to take on still larger dimensions when he bought a financially crippled rail line that ran from Sanford to St. Petersburg. This became part of his growing Atlantic Coast Line Railroad. Then, in 1891, he completed the Tampa Bay Hotel, which was extravagant in size, plan, and furnishings.

Built in two years at a cost of more than $3 million, the Tampa Bay Hotel was at that time the most lavish in Florida. Plant wanted to outdo Flagler, who was building railroads and hotels down Florida's east coast. Tampa at that time had a population of less than 6,000, but Plant turned the opening of his hotel into an international affair by inviting European royalty as well as national dignitaries. In addition to the dinners, parties, and other functions that marked the occasion, guests were treated to performances by a symphony orchestra.

The hotel occupied a 20-acre site in the middle of the budding city, and it was spectacular for its Moorish architecture, with 12 domed towers and bulbous minarets topped with silver crescents. During the Spanish-American War, Teddy Roosevelt and other officers used the Tampa Bay Hotel as headquarters in putting together their army of invasion. Today it houses the University of Tampa.

Henry Plant is sometimes called the "founder of Tampa." True, the town existed before his arrival, but it was Henry Plant who boosted it into prominence and prosperity.

MARJORIE KINNAN RAWLINGS worried that she would be remembered only as a chronicler of backwoods Florida, and this is in fact the identification label she wears. But she is remembered appreciatively for work done magnificently. Though she did not want to be called a regionalist, no one knows her otherwise. She dealt knowingly and lovingly with a wild and natural Florida. She saw oneness in the plants, animals, land, and people and introduced the world to this fascinating bit of America that they probably never would have known otherwise and surely would not have understood.

Born in Washington, D.C. in 1896, Marjorie Kinnan Rawlings began writing when she was six years old. At age 11, she won a writing contest and had her story published in the *Washington Post*. At the University of Wisconsin, she majored in English and was an honor student. Shortly after graduation she married Charles A. Rawlings, whom she had known as a fellow student at the university, and they lived and worked as journalists in his home town of Rochester, New York.

Marjorie Kinnan Rawlings saw Florida for the first time on a vacation trip in 1928 and made a decision then to make it her home. With her husband, she bought a 72-acre citrus grove on Cross Creek in the northern central part of the state. There she blossomed. She was a northerner in Florida cracker (backwoodsman) country, but she won their complete acceptance. She learned their language, and she also lived with them, going for weeks into the Big Scrub country to do what they did for survival and for pleasure.

Five years after buying the grove at Cross Creek, she divorced

Charles Rawlings, who did not adapt to the Florida way of life as she had and who returned north. Marjorie stayed at Cross Creek. That same year — in 1933 — her first book on Florida was published. Called *South Moon Under*, it became a Book-of-the-Month Club selection. Marjorie Kinnan Rawlings was not a Floridian, but *South Moon Under* glued her in the minds of people as being one. Her second and less well known book was *Golden Apples*, published in 1935.

Her third and best-known novel was *The Yearling*, a heart-warming story about a boy and a deer that was published in 1938. It was also a Book-of-the-Month Club selection and was purchased by MGM to be made into a movie, which was not completed and released until 1946. In the interim, Marjorie Kinnan Rawlings was granted the Pulitzer Prize for *The Yearling*, and she received two honorary doctorates — one from Rollins College and the other from the University of Florida.

Marjorie Kinnan Rawlings continued to write, and in 1942 *Cross Creek*, her autobiography, was published. She was awarded another doctorate, this time from the University of Tampa. A year earlier, in 1941, she had married again. Her husband, Norton Sanford Baskin, was in the hotel business, and she moved with him to St. Augustine. Now unaccustomed to city life, however, she continued her sojourns into the back country and, sadly, she became increasingly shy and introvertive as the years went by.

JOHN RINGLING

JOHN RINGLING helped turn tiny Sarasota, along Florida's lower southwest coast, into a thriving tourist town. In the beginning, he spent only his winters there. People from other circuses had discovered Sarasota, and when John Ringling heard their enthusiastic talk about the little town, he decided to give it a try. He went there the first time in 1909. Sarasota then had roughly a thousand inhabitants. About half of them made their livings as fishermen; the others were cattlemen. John Ringling was there to enjoy the sunshine and warm winter weather.

The Ringlings were strong family people, and because he liked Sarasota so much, John began luring others of his family to join him. Soon Charles, Alfred, and Albert were in Sarasota, too. Henry, the fifth brother making up the original Ringling Brothers circus team, established his winter home in Eustis, some one hundred miles to the north. All were far from their native Wisconsin.

The Ringlings were by now accustomed to calling home wherever they happened to be at the moment. They had been "bitten" by the circus bug years earlier when a circus came to MacGregor, Iowa, the town in which they were living at that time. Circus day in any town in America was the biggest event of the year. Cotton candy, lemonade, clowns, trained seals, trapeze performers, ferocious lions and tigers, elephants — a circus fired imaginations, and for the Ringling brothers, it stirred them into deciding to become circus people themselves.

Within a year they had put together a show of their own and had set out performing from town to town, sometimes with success, but just as often with booing receptions to their performance. But they persisted and continued to get better and better. By horse and wagon and sometimes by train, they had traveled more than 8,000 miles and had given some 1,000 performances before they could afford an elephant, the symbol of a circus. Within ten years they had grown to a size demanding 18 train cars to haul their show. Now, too, they boasted three elephants. By the time John Ringling went to Sarasota, they had become a phenomenal success, and already they owned the Barnum and Bailey Circus as well as their own. In 1918, the two were combined to create the giant of the circus business: Ringling Brothers and Barnum & Bailey. It was indeed as they boasted — the Greatest Show on Earth.

By this time, the Ringling brothers were reduced to two — John and Charles. Their other brothers had died. John and Charles began boosting Sarasota. They knew the most influential people in the country, and they were themselves among the richest men in the world. Their homes alone were sights to behold. John's *Ca'd'Zan*, meaning House of John, was a veritable palace, patterned after similar palatial abodes that he and his wife, Mabel, admired in Venice. It cost $1.5 million to build, and this was before 1930. More than 200 feet long and with 30 rooms, it had round-arched windows, a tower with an open balcony that ran all the way around it, large columns, a huge ballroom with an organ, tremendous chandeliers and tapestries — all in all a stupendous extravaganza. On the expansive grounds there were magnificent statues shaded by huge banyan trees and other plants that smacked of the tropics.

Long before his death, John had arranged to have his house deeded to the state of Florida. With it, too, was his similarly extravagant museum in which he kept art masterpieces that he collected from around the world. Even in the 1930s, the building and its collection was valued at more than $15 million. Today the 38-acre complex, which now also includes a collection of circus memorabilia, is a popular tourist attraction.

John Ringling was more flamboyant and venturesome than his brother Charles, but both became involved in civic affairs and in real estate ventures in Sarasota and the surrounding area. John Ringling, for example, bought all of the keys, or little islands, directly in front of Sarasota. Each fronted the Gulf of Mexico and had a magnificent view and beach. He also owned thousands of acres inland.

When Charles died in 1926, John continued to administrate the circus and to pile fortune upon fortune. The depression that came in the late 1920s devastated Florida's real estate and tourism. John Ringling suffered, too, but he shrewdly calculated a way to rescue Sarasota. Until then the big circus had been wintered in Bridgeport, Connecticut. Keeping the animals warm there in winter was both difficult and costly. It was also a time of year when the circus was all expense and no income. John Ringling announced in 1927 that the circus would thereafter be quartered in Sarasota in the winter. It would mean steady work for some of the Sarasota residents. Tourists would be attracted — and would pay — to see the circus all winter long. The animals would be more comfortable in their warmer surroundings.

Sarasota was elated, for having the Greatest Show on Earth move to town was salvation at a time of great need. John Ringling was right, too, for people did indeed flock to Sarasota strictly because of the circus. The biggest event of the year was when the circus put everything together to go on the road in the spring. The circus owned its own railroad cars; the railroad company furnished only the engine, caboose, and track. What a sight! Now there were as many as 90 cars, all of them a bit longer than the standard railroad car. Many had to be specially designed. Giraffes, for example, needed extra neck room. Elephants had to have stronger floors and sides. Lions and tigers rode in cars with bars at the sides. Seals and hippopotamuses needed tanks. The Big Top itself was a gargantuan hunk of freight. There were special cars, too, for the human performers, from the clowns and trapeze artists to those whose main job was putting it all together and then taking it apart swiftly and without mistakes.

Everybody in town gathered at the station to see the circus off for its season on the road, and they were there again to welcome it back when winter winds began to blow. Even today in Sarasota, more than half a century after John Ringling's death, the Ringling mark has not been erased. The buildings and treasures the Ringlings left there are monuments that have inscribed their name in the area for all time.

DAVID LEVY YULEE

DAVID LEVY YULEE went originally by the name of David Levy. Yulee was his father's name, but his mother's maiden name was Levy. On his father's side of the family, he was Portuguese and Mohammedan; on his mother's side, English and Jewish. His name was legally changed to Yulee before his marriage so that his wife — the daughter of a former governor of Kentucky — could justifiably claim that she was married to a gentile.

Born on the island of St. Thomas in the West Indies in 1810, David Levy came to the United States with his family when he was very young. He lived first in Norfolk, Virginia, then later on his father's plantation near St. Augustine in Florida. He was educated in Norfolk, where he also studied law. He was admitted to the bar and became a practicing attorney. At an early age, however, he entered politics. In 1841, David Yulee became a delegate to the United States Congress from the territory of Florida. In 1845 he was elected as one of the first two senators from the new state of Florida.

When the Civil War appeared imminent, David Yulee moved his family to Homosassa, where he felt they would be safe. He had run for and won a senate seat for the second time and served from 1855 until he withdrew in 1861, just eleven days after Florida seceded from the Union. While he was still in Washington, however, Yulee and his companion Florida senator were sending information about the federal government's activities to Governor Perry in Florida. They recommended taking over government-held properties in Florida and the South — by force if necessary. Later he denied his role as a conspirator, but as soon as he left Washington, he turned his energies to helping the Confederacy and also served on its congress.

At the end of the war, David Yulee was imprisoned at Fort Pulaski near Savannah, Georgia. He was charged with conspiracy and also aiding in the escape of Jefferson Davis. Foes wanted him executed, but in the spring of 1866, after serving about six months, he was pardoned by President Ulysses S. Grant and released.

David Yulee was active also in the economic development of Florida. He was president of the Florida Railroad, which connected Fernandina, immediately north of Jacksonville, with Cedar Key on the upper Gulf coast. His railroad and Cedar Key were targets of Union attacks during the war.

It was soon after his release from prison that Republicans in Florida accused David Yulee of influencing the votes of his employees — more specifically, of personally providing them with already-marked ballots. The Republicans seemed to feel that this was not in the true spirit of the democratic election process, especially since none of the names on the ballots were of Republican candidates. Yulee responded that the charge was "unfounded and untrue." He added, in a very carefully worded statement, that if his company *had* done as accused, it would only have been doing what it had a right to do, because it was justified in taking whatever actions necessary to ensure its own financial survival and protection. In David Yulee's opinion, if that meant a little extra help for politicians that were friendly to Yulee's company, well, he and the company were free to give it. With such an attitude, it's not hard to understand why David Yulee was a colorful, controversial character in the state.

In 1900, David Yulee moved to Washington, D.C. Six years later he died of a bronchial cold in the Clarendon Hotel in New York City. He was buried in a cemetery in Washington.

Levy County, on the upper Gulf coast of Florida, is named after David Levy Yulee.

FOR MORE ABOUT FLORIDIANS

Listed here are a few references that may be both interesting and helpful as you explore more deeply the history of Florida and its people. You may find additional references dealing with a particular person's life, or you may get specific information from encyclopedias, some of which deal exclusively with biographies.

Bamford, Hal. *Florida History.* Great Outdoors Publishing Company, St. Petersburg, Florida, 1976.

Copeland, L. S. and J. E. Dovell. *La Florida.* Steck-Vaughn Company, Austin, Texas, 1957.

Curl, Donald Walter. *Mizner's Florida.* MIT Press, Cambridge, Massachusetts, 1984.

Douglas, Marjorie Stoneman and John Rothchild. *Marjorie Stoneman Douglas,* Pineapple Press, Sarasota, Florida, 1987.

Dunn, Hampton. *Florida: A Pictorial History.* The Donning Company, Norfolk Beach, Virginia, 1988.

Florida, (WPA Guide), Pantheon Books, New York, 1984.

Morris, Allen. *The Florida Handbook, 1989-1990.* Peninsular Publishing Company, Tallahassee, Florida, 1989.

North, Henry Ringling. *The Circus Kings.* Doubleday, New York, 1960.

Tebeau, Charlton W. *Florida from Indian Trail to Space Age.* (3 volumes) The Southern Publishing Company, Delray Beach, Florida, 1965.

Wagy, Tom R. *Governor LeRoy Collins of Florida.* The University of Alabama Press, 1985.